CONTENTS

Sections marked with this symbol have free audio clips available at www.franklinwatts.co.uk/downloads

Ryan

MEET RYAN, OUR YOUNG REPORTER IN FRANCE

Meet Ryan. He is in France on a special mission. He is going to find out about French children, their homes and their families. He has lots of questions.

How many people are there in a typical French family?

What are French children's favourite pets?

What do French families do when they're together?

What do French children like eating?

What's a typical French house like?

What is there for children to do in French towns?

Read on to find out the answers to these questions... *and lots more!*

BIENVENUE EN FRANCE!

CREST •

The little town of Crest is in south-east France. Meet some children who live there.

Antoine is 11.

He lives with his mum, his dad, his two sisters and his dog, Bonbon.

He enjoys being with his family and loves going to see his grandparents.

Find out why!

Antoine

Léo is 9.

He lives in Crest with his family.

He loves Crest and all the sports he can do there.

Find out which is his favourite shop in town.

Léo

Did you know?

On average, a French person has 30 close relatives.

Juliette is 12.

Her parents are divorced. She lives with her dad and younger brother, Jérémie.

They have a very large house. Come and have a look round!

Juliette

You can practise your French and learn some new words as you find out what these children have to say.

VOICI MA FAMILLE!

Today our young reporter is interviewing Antoine about his family.

Young reporter: **Salut, Antoine! Il y a qui dans ta famille?**

Antoine: **Dans ma famille, il y a ma mère, mon père et mes sœurs, Loriane et Pauline.**

The average French family has at least two children. After Ireland, France is the country with the most children (**les enfants**) per family in Europe. So Antoine's family is quite typical! Their family name is Corsini. It was originally an Italian name: Antoine's grandad came to France from Italy after the Second World War (1939–45). About a quarter of French people have a parent or grandparent that came from abroad, often from Portugal, Spain, Italy or North Africa.

J'ai un chien. Il s'appelle Bonbon. J'adore mon chien!

À Crest, il y a aussi mon grand-père et ma grand-mère. Ils sont super!

USEFUL PHRASES

Salut, Antoine! Hi, Antoine!　**dans ma famille** in my family　**il y a** there is/there are **aussi** too　**mon père** my father　**ma mère** my mother　**mes sœurs** my sisters **mon grand-père** my grandfather　**ma grand-mère** my grandmother **ils sont super** they're great　**j'ai un chien** I have a dog　**il s'appelle** he's called

Antoine hasn't got a big extended family as his mum is an only child. His father has a brother, so he has an uncle (**un oncle**), an aunt (**une tante**) and two cousins (**deux cousins**) he sees quite often. Like many children in France, Antoine has a godfather (**un parrain**) and a godmother (**une marraine**). They would look after him should anything happen to his mum and dad.

Antoine gets on very well with his sisters, but he would

Hugo joins in with a family celebration.

have loved a brother (**un frère**) as well. Luckily, Hugo, Loriane's boyfriend (**le petit copain**), joins in most family celebrations. He and Antoine are really good friends.

Antoine says, "**Mes parents sont super sympa!**" His mum and dad are really great. Antoine gets on well with his dad as they both love football. His mum can be a bit

strict but not too often – and she said yes to him adopting a pet (**un animal domestique**) from a rescue centre! His pet dog Bonbon is now four and Antoine loves him to bits.

Bonbon likes fooling around with Antoine!

Family members

my father (**mon père**)   my mother (**ma mère**)   my brother (**mon frère**)   my sister (**ma sœur**)   my grandfather (**mon grand-père**)   my grandmother (**ma grand-mère**)   my uncle (**mon oncle**)   my aunt (**ma tante**)   my cousin (**mon cousin/ma cousine**)   my step-father (**mon beau-père**)   my step-mother (**ma belle-mère**)   my step-brother (**mon demi-frère**)   my step-sister (**ma demi-sœur**)

YOUR TURN

Et toi, il y a qui dans ta famille?

 Dans ma famille, il y a...

Children's names for family members:
Mum = **Maman**
Dad = **Papa**
Granny/Nan = **Mamie (or Mémé)**
Grandad = **Papy (or Pépé)**
Uncle = **Tonton**
Aunt = **Tatie (or Tata)**

FAMILY FACTS

For the majority of French people, family is the most important thing in their lives.

What's in a name?

Surnames (**les noms de famille**) date back to the Middle Ages (5th to the 15th century), when France's population was growing rapidly. Before that, people had just a first name (**le prénom**). At first, nicknames were used: for instance, **Petit**, if you were short, **Legrand**, if you were tall.

The ten most common surnames in modern France are: Martin, Bernard, Dubois, Thomas, Robert, Richard, Petit, Durand, Leroy and Moreau.

First names go in and out of fashion. The most fashionable now are: Enzo, Lucas, Nathan, Mathis and Louis for boys. For girls they are: Emma, Léa, Clara, Chloé and Manon.

Did you know?

Mon Oncle (1958) is a great old film by French actor and director Jacques Tati, about an eccentric uncle, his nephew and lots of little dogs! It's very visual and easy to follow.

Love and kisses

French people tend to kiss (**faire la bise**) a lot. Family members kiss each other on the cheek at least twice a day, morning and night, and friends kiss when they meet. The number of kisses may vary from one to four, depending on local traditions. It can be quite confusing!

Long live Granny!

In the whole of Europe, it is French women who live longest, so there are lots of grandmas in France... seven million of them! Their special day is on the first Sunday in March, **la Fête des Grand-mères**. On average, they have five grandchildren (**les petits-enfants**). Children whose parents work or are divorced are often looked after by their grandparents.

Did you know?

The French hold the European record for having the most pets. Yet, many animals are abandoned at the start of the summer holidays, a busy time for France's animal protection agency: **la SPA**.

MINI-QUIZ

Can you guess the correct answers?

1 What are the top three pets in France?

- **le chat** (cat)
- **le hamster** (hamster)
- **le chien** (dog)
- **le furet** (ferret)

2 Which first names are for both boys and girls?

- Camille, Lou, Maxence
- Martine, Audrey, Laurence
- Frédéric, Nicolas, Jean

3 Which family celebration takes place in May?

- **la Fête des Grand-mères**
- **la Fête des Mères**
- **la Fête des Pères**

MINI-QUIZ ANSWERS

3 la Fête des Mères

2 Camille, Lou, Maxence

1 le chien, le chat, le furet

EXTRA CHALLENGE

Design your own family tree: stick photos or drawings of your family and label them in French.

UN WEEK-END EN FAMILLE

Our young reporter asks Antoine to tell him about a typical weekend at home.

Young reporter: **C'est comment, le week-end, chez toi?**

Antoine: **Le samedi, je fais mes devoirs et j'aide à la maison.**

Le dimanche, on joue ou on fait une sortie en famille.

J'aide Maman à la maison.

If Saturday is usually a day for chores – shopping (**les courses**), housework (**le ménage**) and homework – Sunday is for relaxing and spending time together. After a lazy morning lie-in (**une grasse matinée**), the whole family gathers for Sunday lunch, followed by TV, games or an outing, depending on the weather. Antoine's family love to play old-fashioned board games (**des jeux de société**).

On joue en famille.

USEFUL PHRASES

C'est comment, le week-end, chez toi? What's the weekend like at your home?
le samedi on Saturdays **le dimanche** on Sundays **Je fais mes devoirs** I do my homework
J'aide à la maison I help with the housework **on joue** we play **ou** or
on fait une sortie we go on an outing **en famille** with the whole family

MY BLOG

Antoine's family, like most French families, take the weekend very seriously. The parents work hard all week and his sisters only come home for the weekend – they go to university in Grenoble from Monday to Friday. The family eat all their meals (**les repas**) together around the table. That's when they catch up on each other's news.

Many French families visit grandparents (**les grands-parents**) on Sundays. Antoine's grandma and grandad live just outside Crest. They have a house with a huge garden, swings (**des balançoires**) and a fantastic swimming pool (**une piscine**). Antoine has none of that at home as he lives in an old flat in Crest town centre, so it's always a treat to visit his grandparents. He sometimes takes friends or meets up with his cousins.

Antoine says: "**J'aide Papy au jardin. C'est génial!**" He loves nature and helping his grandad in the garden. Gardening is among the favourite weekend pastimes for parents and grandparents in France.

Weekend activities

I help (**j'aide**)   with housework (**au ménage**)   with the cooking (**à la cuisine**)   with the shopping (**aux courses**)   with the gardening (**au jardin**)   we have a lie-in (**on fait la grasse matinée**)   we go out (**on fait une sortie**)   we visit my grandparents (**on va voir mes grands-parents**)   we play (**on joue**)   we watch TV (**on regarde la télé**)   we eat together (**on mange ensemble**)   we chat (**on discute**)

YOUR TURN

Et toi, c'est comment le week-end, chez toi?

Chez moi, le samedi...
Le dimanche...

Listen to and practise the French 'on' sound. Try saying 'oh' but with your nose and throat.

Dressed-up for a wedding

What is family life like in France?

French children spend a lot of time with their parents every day, especially at mealtimes when they sit, eat and talk together. They also help with the family meal, mostly laying the table (**mettre le couvert**) and clearing it (**débarrasser**).

French families are usually quite close and spend as much time as possible together, especially at weekends. That's regardless of whether they stay at home, go to their second home (when they have one) or stay with family and friends.

Families also enjoy getting together for special occasions or major events too, such as weddings (**les mariages**), baptisms (**les baptêmes**), communions (**les communions**) or wedding anniversaries (**les anniversaires de mariage**).

Did you know?

It is traditional in France to give sugared almonds (**des dragées**) to guests at christenings, communions and weddings.

What do French children do? With whom?
Top 12

(1)	Television	La télévision
(2)	Reading	La lecture
(3)	Internet	L'internet
(4)	Music	La musique
(5)	Video games	Les jeux vidéo
(6)	Cooking	La cuisine
(7)	Sports	Les sports
(8)	Board games	Les jeux de société
(9)	DIY	Le bricolage
(10)	Shopping	Le shopping
(11)	Outings	Les sorties
(12)	Religious activities	Les activités religieuses

with the father (**avec le père**)

with the mother (**avec la mère**)

with the grandparents (**avec les grands-parents**)

Generally, it is mothers who read with their children and help out with homework. Children in primary school have about 15 minutes' homework every day. Children in secondary school have much more – 35 minutes to an hour. Most French children – 96% – do their homework as soon as they get home. Do you?

Fathers are more often involved in sports, television, video games and DIY. DIY is the main hobby for 80% of French men and 50% of women.

At weekends, it's very common to see whole families in out-of-town shopping centres (**les centres commerciaux**), stocking up in DIY stores (**les magasins de bricolage**) and doing their weekly shopping in giant supermarkets (**les hypermarchés**).

MINI-QUIZ

Can you guess?

1 Which French shop is not a DIY store?

- Bricorama
- Mr. Bricolage
- Intermarché

2 What is **un livre de cuisine**?

- a kitchen catalogue
- a recipe book
- kitchen scales

3 What do people say to each other before the weekend?

- **Bonne chance!**
- **Bon week-end!**
- **À vos souhaits!**

MINI-QUIZ ANSWERS

1 Intermarché (supermarket)
2 Recipe book
3 **Bon week-end!** (the others mean 'Good luck' and 'Bless you')

EXTRA CHALLENGE

Compare your weekend with a typical French weekend.

What's similar? What's different?

À TABLE!

Today, Ryan is finding out about mealtimes and asks Juliette what she eats at home.

Young reporter: **Qu'est-ce que tu manges le matin? le midi ? le soir ?**

Juliette: **Le matin, je mange du pain, avec du beurre et de la confiture.**

Le midi, je mange à la cantine.

Le soir, je mange de la viande ou du poisson, des légumes et des fruits.

Le petit déjeuner avec Papa et mon frère.

Did you know?

In France, it's not bad manners to dunk your bread in a hot drink.

Juliette thinks breakfast (**le petit déjeuner**) is a very important meal. It gives her and her brother a chance to chat with their dad. They don't see him at lunchtime (**le déjeuner**), as they stay at school and eat at the canteen, and he often comes back from work too late to have dinner (**le dîner**) with them.

Juliette's dad likes getting the bread fresh from the bakery (**la boulangerie**) before the children wake up. When they get up, they are greeted by a lovely smell of fresh bread and coffee (**le café**) or hot chocolate (**le chocolat chaud**).

USEFUL PHRASES

Qu'est-ce que tu manges? What do you eat? **le matin** for breakfast **le midi** for lunch **le soir** for dinner **je mange** I eat **du pain** bread **avec du beurre et de la confiture** with butter and jam **à la cantine** at the canteen **de la viande** meat **du poisson** fish **des légumes** vegetables **des fruits** fruit

MY BLOG

Juliette loves breakfast, and also **le goûter**, the snack many French children have when they come back from school. Juliette and Jérémie have biscuits (**des biscuits**) and a chocolate-filled pastry (**un petit pain au chocolat**).

The other important meal in a French home is dinner (**le dîner**). This is usually the main meal of the day with a starter, generally soup (**de la soupe**), salad (**une salade**) or some cold meats (**de la charcuterie**), then a dish of meat or fish with vegetables, rice (**du riz**) or pasta (**des pâtes**) followed by a dessert: fruit, cake (**un gâteau**) or yoghurt (**un yaourt**).

Juliette is a very good cook. She can even cook some of the local specialities. She made semolina sausages (**quenelles lyonnaises**) with vol au vents (**bouchées à la reine**) for dinner tonight and bought a special local bread called focaccia (**une fougasse**).

Juliette drinks mineral water or fruit juice with her dinner. Jérémie prefers fruit squash (**le sirop de fruit**).

Juliette says: "**Mon plat préféré, c'est la quiche Lorraine.**" Her favourite dish is quiche Lorraine, a flan made from eggs, ham or bacon and cheese. What's yours?

French children's favourite food

steak and chips (**un steak-frites**)   chicken and chips (**un poulet-frites**)
ham and mashed potato (**un jambon-purée**)   cottage pie (**un hachis parmentier**)
a burger (**un hamburger**)   a pizza (**une pizza**)   a paella (**une paella**)
spring rolls (**des nems**)   vegetable stew (**une ratatouille**)   lasagna (**des lasagnes**)

YOUR TURN

Et toi, qu'est-ce que tu manges le matin? le midi? le soir?

 Le matin, je mange…
Le midi, …   Le soir, …

To say, "Enjoy your meal!" say: "**Bon appétit!**" To say you enjoyed a meal, say: "**C'était très bon, merci!**"

FRENCH FOOD

Mealtimes are important occasions in France.

Eating in

Four out of five French families eat their meals together at the dining table. Some might watch TV at the same time, but TV dinners on a tray are not at all popular.

A typical Sunday meal can go on for hours, especially if it is shared with family

Some family meals can be very long!

and friends! It will start with a pre-meal drink (**un apéritif**), then a starter (**une entrée**), followed by a main course (**un plat principal**), a green salad (**de la salade**), then some cheese (**du fromage**) and finally, after a break, a dessert (**un dessert**) and coffee. Children are generally allowed to leave the table and come back for dessert!

It is not unusual for friends to be invited just for drinks or the dessert, rather than for the whole meal.

Did you know?

There are over 400 different French cheeses: you could eat a different one every day for a year and still not have tried them all!

Cheeses are often called after the place where they are made: **Roquefort, Brie** etc.

Eating out

The French also love eating out on Sundays, for birthdays, Mother's Day and other occasions. The first ever restaurant (**un restaurant**) opened in Paris in 1765. Most restaurants offer traditional French cuisine but food from other countries is also very popular, especially North African food such as meat and vegetable stew served with couscous (made from semolina). There is often a children's menu (**un menu enfant**) but, on the whole, French children are quite adventurous and will eat dishes from the main menu.

You'll find McDonalds in most large cities but France also has its own fast food chains, which are adapted to French taste such as **Quick, Flunch**, **Paul** and **la Brioche Dorée**.

La semaine du goût

Every year, French children learn about food in their schools with well-known chefs and other professionals (bakers, cake-makers, chocolate makers). They taste lots of lovely food and are encouraged to eat healthily at home.

MINI-QUIZ

Can you guess what these mean?

1 What will you eat if you're offered '**des fruits de mer**'?
- seafood
- dried fruit
- fruit salad

2 Which is the French word for snails?
- **des escargots**
- **des grenouilles**
- **des huîtres**

3 Which food makes the French town of Camembert famous?
- bread
- cheese
- mustard

MINI-QUIZ ANSWERS

1 seafood

2 des escargots (the others are frogs and oysters)

3 cheese

EXTRA CHALLENGE

Can you name three French food specialities?

What is your favourite French food?

À LA MAISON

Today Juliette is showing our young reporter around the house she lives in with her dad and brother.

Young reporter: **C'est comment, chez toi?**

Juliette: **Avec Papa, j'habite dans une maison à Crest. Avec Maman, j'habite dans un appartement à Hyères.**

Le salon

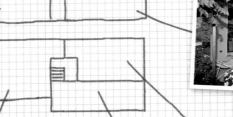

La salle à manger

Le plan de ma maison

La cuisine

Ma chambre

La terrasse

La chambre de Papa

La salle de bains

La chambre de Jérémie

USEFUL PHRASES

C'est comment, chez toi? What's your home like? **j'habite** I live
dans une maison in a house **dans un appartement** in a flat

Juliette's parents are divorced. She lives with her dad and stays with her mum during the holidays. Her dad's house is typical of the region: the outside is pink and the shutters (**les volets**) are blue. It is a T5, which means it has five main rooms (**les pièces**) plus a kitchen and a bathroom/toilet. Juliette's bedroom is on the ground floor (**au rez-de-chaussée**). Her brother Jérémie's room – with its very loud drum kit – is on the first floor (**au premier étage**). The shaded patio and the garden are great in summer.

Juliette loves her bedroom. In it, she has a bed (**un lit**), a desk (**un bureau**), a chair (**une chaise**) and a wardrobe (**une armoire**). Juliette says: "**Dans ma chambre, il y a aussi mes peluches!**" She also has all her cuddly toys in her bedroom. She's been collecting them for years. And, of course, there is Princesse, her cat, who has a little bed of her own!

In a French home

sitting room (**un salon**) dining room (**une salle à manger**)
kitchen (**une cuisine**) bedroom (**une chambre**) study (**un bureau**)
bathroom (**une salle de bains**) toilet (**des toilettes**)
patio (**une terrasse**) balcony (**un balcon**) attic (**un grenier**)
cellar (**une cave**) garage (**un garage**) garden (**un jardin**)

YOUR TURN

Et toi? C'est comment, chez toi?

- *J'habite dans …*
- *Il y a …*

In French, you don't sound the 'h'. Have a go at this tongue twister!

Henri le hamster habite à Hyères.

FRENCH HOMES

French people spend a lot of money on their homes, more than on food!

Typical homes

French houses look very different depending on where you are in the country: for instance, in Brittany in north-west France, a typical house is white, with stone edging around the doors and windows and a grey slate roof (above). In Normandy and Alsace, houses are half-timbered (middle left). In Southern France, roofs are covered with red tiles. In the mountains, there are wooden chalets (bottom right).

Second homes

More people in France own a second home (**une résidence secondaire**) than anywhere else in the world: often it used to belong to parents or grandparents and is used for weekends and holidays. It is usually an old farm (**une ferme**) or a house by the sea (**une villa**). Houses with swimming pools are common in southern France where the weather is warm.

Unfortunately, some people in France don't have a home at all: they are called **les SDF**, which means **sans domicile fixe**, without a fixed address. There are more than 500,000 children without a proper home in France.

Did you know?

Le Château de Versailles is the most famous and luxurious home ever built in France. King Louis XIV built this palace close to Paris in the 17th century. It is one of the most visited places in France.

A French invention: the 'green' house

This revolutionary house, called Domespace (above), was invented by a French company in 1988.

It is very ecologically friendly. It is made of wood and rotates to follow the sun.

MINI-QUIZ

Can you guess?

1 Which of these famous Paris monuments used to be the French king's home before Versailles?

- **Notre-Dame de Paris**
- **Le Louvre**
- **L'Arc de Triomphe**

2 Which of these places is home to the President of the French Republic?

- **le Palais de Versailles**
- **le Palais de l'Élysée**
- **le Stade de France**

3 Which is the sign for bed and breakfast in France?

- **Maison d'arrêt**
- **Hôtel de ville**
- **Chambre d'hôte**

MINI-QUIZ ANSWERS

1 Le Louvre

2 le Palais de l'Élysée

3 Chambre d'hôte (the other two mean prison and town hall)

EXTRA CHALLENGE

Draw a plan of your house or your flat and label the different rooms in French.

EN VILLE

Our young reporter asks Léo what there is to do or see in his home town.

Young reporter: **Salut, Léo. Qu'est-ce qu'il y a dans ta ville?**

Léo: **Ici, il y a plein de choses! Il y a un centre sportif, il y a une piscine, il y a des magasins. Moi, j'adore Crest!**

PARC DU BOSQUET

Il y a un parc avec des jeux, c'est super!

Crest is a small medieval town that attracts lots of tourists in the summer. Léo has visited the tower (**la tour**) a few times. It is the highest dungeon in France and has great views from the top. Crest also has the longest wooden bridge in France!

The streets are busy and narrow with shops (**des magasins**), various markets (**des marchés**) and lots of festivals (**des festivals**).

Note – the 'st' of Crest is not pronounced, so it sounds like 'cray'.

USEFUL PHRASES

Qu'est-ce qu'il y a? What is there?   **dans ta ville** in your town   **ici** here
il y a plein de choses there are lots of things   **un centre sportif** a sports centre
une piscine a swimming pool   **des magasins** shops   **un parc** a park
avec des jeux with a playground

Crest is small enough for Léo and his friends to be able to walk to the centre. Léo makes good use of the sports facilities: there is a climbing wall (**un mur d'escalade**), tennis courts (**des courts de tennis**), a crazy golf course (**un mini-golf**), a swimming pool (**une piscine**) and there is also a river (**une rivière**) where he swims and goes canoeing in the summer.

Crest has a good cinema (**un cinéma**) where Léo enjoys going with his brother. They both love cartoons. His mum sometimes takes him to the

Visit Crest in a horse-drawn carriage.

library (**la bibliothèque**) and to the toy library (**la ludothèque**) where he can borrow toys and board games. There are also great shows for children (**des spectacles pour enfants**) in the

community centre (**la salle des fêtes**).

When I asked Léo about his favourite place in Crest, he replied: "**Mon endroit préféré, c'est le magasin de bonbons!**" His favourite place is the sweet shop!

Here Léo is in heaven!

Places in a French town

bus stop (**l'arrêt de bus**)   playground (**l'aire de jeux**)   bank (**la banque**)
railway station (**la gare**)   hotel (**l'hôtel**)   museum (**le musée**)
tourist office (**l'office du tourisme**)   supermarket (**le supermarché**)
car park (**le parking**)   chemist (**la pharmacie**)   harbour (**le port**)
beach (**la plage**)   post office (**la poste**)   restaurant (**le restaurant**)

Il y a is very useful: it means both 'there is' and 'there are'.

YOUR TURN

Et toi, qu'est-ce qu'il y a dans ta ville?

☺ *Dans ma ville, il y a …*

← Temple - Eglise
← Hôtel de Ville
← Police Municipale
← Office de Tourisme

AROUND TOWN

Here are some facts about French towns.

Flats in a city centre

Town or country

Before 1945, most people in France lived in the country (**à la campagne**). Now, most live in or outside a town (**en ville**). Richer people tend to live in city centres (**au centre-ville**) or in large houses far out in smart suburbs (**en banlieue**). Less well-off people are more likely to live just outside of towns, on housing estates (**les cités**) and in high-rise buildings called **les HLM**.

Flats in a suburb

Saint-Malo: a walled city by the sea

Old towns and cities

Most old French cities were built near the sea, along rivers, in agricultural or industrial areas. They were usually built around a castle (**un château**) or a cathedral (**une cathédrale**). A lot of towns have a bypass (**une rocade**) to take traffic away from narrow city centre streets that are kept for pedestrians (**les rues piétonnières**). Few have large parks, but most have several playgrounds for children.

Dinan: an old town with narrow streets

France is constantly trying to improve transport in towns, making it more environmentally-friendly. New trains run in the Paris metro (**le métro**) and there are more and more new trams (**les trams**), bike-hire schemes (**les vélos à la carte**) and rickshaws (**les vélo-taxis**).

Did you know?

The French town with the shortest name is Y.

The longest is Saint-Remy-en-Bouzemont-Saint-Genest-et-Isson.

A sign at the roadside tells you the name of the town you are entering. When you leave, the sign is crossed out.

There are over 36,700 French towns.

The five largest (in order of size) are: Paris, Marseille, Lyon, Toulouse and Nice (above).

The capital city is Paris.

The oldest city is Marseille (founded 600 BCE).

La promenade des Anglais, Nice

MINI-QUIZ

1 Match each town with its football team.

Paris	OM
Marseille	OL
Lyon	PSG

2 Complete the name of the town in this traditional song.

Sur le pont d' _____
On y danse, on y danse,
Sur le pont d' _____
On y danse tous en rond.

- Lyon
- Avignon
- Toulon

MINI-QUIZ ANSWERS

2 Avignon

PSG = Paris
OL = Lyon
1 OM = Marseille

EXTRA CHALLENGE

How many French towns can you name?

What do you know about each one?

TEST YOUR MEMORY!

1 What is the word French children use for 'mum'?

- **Mamie**
- **Mémé**
- **Maman**

2 What do children help with most at home?

- cooking
- cleaning
- laying and clearing the table

3 What is the most common thing for French children to do with both their mum and dad?

- watch TV
- play board games
- DIY

4 What is 'le petit déjeuner'?

- an after school snack
- a light lunch
- breakfast

5 What is a typical French Sunday meal?

- apéritif, starter, main course, salad, cheese, dessert, coffee
- apéritif, main course, dessert, coffee
- main course, dessert, cheese

6 What is the French word for swimming pool?

- **une salle de bains**
- **une piscine**
- **une rivière**

7 Where are you most likely to see grey slate roofs?

- In northern France
- In southern France
- In the mountains

8 What is the largest French city after Paris?

- Lyon
- Marseille
- Toulouse

Look back through the book to check your answers.

INTERESTING WEBSITES

- **Watch a video about French families gathering for special occasions:** http://www.bbc.co.uk/learningzone/clips/family-coming-together-for-celebrations/1056.html
- **Watch a video about two boys at home:** http://www.bbc.co.uk/learningzone/clips/chez-moi/1700.html
- **Use videos and games to practise vocabulary related to family and pets:** http://www.bbc.co.uk/schools/primarylanguages/french/families/
- **Play a game to discover and make French recipes:** http://oeufs-asso.com/enfant/jeu1.php
- **Visit the website for the town of Crest:** http://www.mairie-crest.fr/-Decouvrir-.html
- **See Paris as if you were there (360 panoramic photos):** http://www.panoramique-360.com/virtual_tour_paris_en.htm
- **Find out lots of information about French towns (in both French and English):** http://www.caloundracity.asn.au/Francofiles/villes/ville_index.htm
- **Play a game locating cities on a French map:** http://www.jeux-geographiques.com/jeux-geographiques-Villes-de-France-Junior-_pageid40.html

Note to parents and teachers: Every effort has been made by the Publishers to ensure that these websites are suitable for children, that they are of the highest educational value, and that they contain no inappropriate or offensive material. However, because of the nature of the Internet, it is impossible to guarantee that the contents of these sites will not be altered. We strongly advise that Internet access is supervised by a responsible adult.

TRANSLATIONS

Voici ma famille! Here are my family!

Salut, Antoine! Il y a qui dans ta famille?
Hi Antoine! Who is in your family?

Dans ma famille, il y a ma mère, mon père et mes sœurs Loriane et Pauline.
In my family, there are my mother, my father and my two sisters, Loriane and Pauline.

À Crest, il y a aussi mon grand-père et ma grand-mère. Ils sont super!
In Crest, there are also my grandfather and my grandmother. They're great!

J'ai un chien. Il s'appelle Bonbon. J'adore mon chien!
I have a dog. His name is Bonbon. I love my dog!

Mes parents sont super sympa!
My parents are really nice.

Et toi, il y a qui dans ta famille?
What about you? Who's in your family?

Dans ma famille, il y a…
In my family, there are…

Pages 12–13

Un week-end en famille A family weekend

C'est comment, le week-end, chez toi?
What's the weekend like at your home?

Le samedi, je fais mes devoirs et j'aide à la maison.
On Saturdays, I do my homework and I help with the housework.

Le dimanche, on joue ou on fait une sortie en famille.
On Sundays, we play games or we go on an outing with the whole family.

J'aide Maman à la maison.
I help Mum with the housework.

On joue en famille.
We play with the whole family.

J'aide Papy au jardin. C'est génial!
I help Grandad do the gardening. It's great!

Et toi, c'est comment le week-end, chez toi?
What about you? What's the weekend like at your home?

Chez moi, le samedi,…
At my home, on Saturdays, we…

Le dimanche,… On Sundays,…

Pages 16–17

À table! At the table!

Qu'est-ce que tu manges le matin? le midi? le soir?
What do you eat for breakfast? For lunch? For dinner?

Le matin, je mange du pain, avec du beurre et de la confiture.
For breakfast, I eat bread with butter and jam.

Le midi, je mange à la cantine.
At lunchtime, I eat at the canteen.

Le soir, je mange de la viande ou du poisson, des légumes et des fruits.
For dinner, I have meat or fish, vegetables and fruit.

Le petit déjeuner avec Papa et mon frère.
Breakfast with Dad and my brother.

Mon plat préféré, c'est la quiche Lorraine.
My favourite dish is quiche Lorraine.

Et toi, qu'est-ce que tu manges le matin? le midi? le soir?
What about you? What do you eat for breakfast? For lunch? For dinner?

Le matin, je mange… For breakfast, I eat
Le midi,… For lunch/ At lunchtime,…
Le soir,… For dinner,…

Pages 20–21

À la maison At home
C'est comment, chez toi?
What's your home like?

Avec Papa, j'habite dans une maison à Crest.
With Dad, I live in a house in Crest.

Avec Maman, j'habite dans un appartement à Hyères.
With Mum, I live in a flat in Hyères.

Le plan de ma maison The plan of my house

Dans ma chambre, il y a aussi mes peluches.
In my room, there are also my cuddly toys.

Et toi? C'est comment, chez toi?
What about you? What's your home like?

J'habite dans… I live in…

Il y a… There is /are…

Pages 24–25

En ville In the town

Salut Léo. Qu'est-ce qu'il y a dans ta ville?
Hi Léo! What is there in your town?

Ici, il y a plein de choses! Il y a un centre sportif, il y a une piscine, il y a des magasins… Moi, j'adore Crest!
Here, there are lots of things! There is a sports centre, there is a swimming pool, there are shops… Personally, I love Crest!

Il y a un parc avec des jeux. C'est super!
There is a park with a playground. It's great!

Mon endroit préféré, c'est le magasin de bonbons.
My favourite place is the sweet shop.

Et toi, qu'est-ce qu'il y a dans ta ville?
What about you? What is there in your town?

Dans ma ville, il y a…
In my town, there is…

INDEX

TEST YOUR FRENCH

Can you remember what these words mean?

1 un parrain: a father? a grandfather? a godfather?

2 faire les courses: to go to lessons? to go shopping? to run races?

3 le pain: bread? cake? chicken?

4 la salle de bains: bedroom? bathroom? kitchen?

5 des magasins: magazines? shops? museums?

1 a godfather; 2 to go shopping; 3 bread; 4 bathroom; 5 shops